Badgers

Victoria Blakemore

For Nanny Helen, for being there to walk me to the bus stop on my first day of kindergarten and so many other things

Copyright info/picture credits

Cover, Miroslav Hlavko/Shutterstock; Page 3, StefanHoffman/Pixabay; Page 5, Beeki/Pixabay; Page 7, andyballard/Pixabay; Page 9, Storyblocks; Pages 10-11, Storyblocks; Page 13, Beeki/Pixabay; Page 15, Lee Haywood/flickr; Page 17, skeeze/Pixabay; Page 19, wollertz/AdobeStock; Page 21, Jillian/AdobeStock; Page 23; Peter Trimming/flickr; Page 25, Beeki/Pixabay; Page 27, Storyblocks; Page 29, Storyblocks; Page 31, USFWS Mountain-Prairie/flickr; Page 33, Miroslav Hlavko/Shutterstock

Table of Contents

What Are Badgers?

Badgers are small mammals.

They are related to otters,

wolverines, and weasels.

There are seven different

kinds of badgers. They differ

in where they live and their

coloration. Most are brown or

gray with black and white

stripes on their head

The word badger comes from

the French word for digger.

Size

Badgers can grow to be between twenty and thirty-four inches long. Their tail can add up to six more inches to their body length.

When fully grown, badgers often weigh between ten and forty pounds.

Male badgers are usually larger

than female badgers.

Physical Characteristics

Badgers have very loose skin.
They are able to turn around
even if they are grabbed. This
can help them to escape from
predators.

Badgers have very strong paws
with sharp claws. They use them
for digging and self defense.

Badgers have a third eyelid. It protects their eyes from dirt when they are digging.

Habitat

Most badgers are found in open grasslands. They can also live in forests and other wooded areas.

Badgers prefer areas that are usually dry with lots of plants. They need dry ground so that they can dig their burrows.

Range

Badgers are found in North America, Africa, Asia, and Europe.

In the United States, badgers are found in states such as Texas, Utah, Idaho, and Montana.

Diet

Badgers are **omnivores**, which means that they eat meat and plants.

Their diet is mainly made up of rabbits, groundhogs, squirrels, mice, and snakes. They also eat insects and fruit if no other food is around.

Badgers have a very powerful sense of smell. They are able to smell prey through the soil.

Burrows

Badgers use their strong legs and sharp claws to dig burrows. Their burrows are called setts.

Setts often have long tunnels and **chambers** where the badgers sleep. They fill the **chambers** with leaves and grasses for bedding.

Badger setts may have more than one opening. They are connected by tunnels and provide plenty of fresh air.

Communication

Badgers use mainly scent and sound to communicate with each other. They are able to make sounds such as growls, squeaks, barks, and purrs.

Badgers have special scent glands. They can make a very strong scent if they feel **threatened**.

Badgers also use their scent

glands to mark their **territory**.

Movement

Badgers can run at speeds of up to twenty miles per hour. This is only for short distances.

The ferret-badgers of Asia are very good climbers. They have special **ridges** on the bottom of their paws that help them to climb trees.

Badgers are very fast at digging. They can dig through hard, rocky soil.

Badger Cubs

Badgers have between two

and five babies, or cubs.

Their cubs are born blind

with very thin hair.

Cubs are born in a sett. They

stay inside the sett until they

are about eight weeks old.

Then, they are able to go

outside.

Cubs stay with their mothers

until they are about six months

old.

Badger Life

Badgers can be **solitary** animals. They spend most of their time alone. There are some badgers who live in groups called clans.

Badgers can be very **aggressive**. They are likely to attack animals or people who get too close.

Badgers are **nocturnal**. They are

most active at night and sleep

during the day.

The Importance of Badgers

Badgers have a very important job in their ecosystem. They are close to the top of the food chain and prey on many small animals.

By hunting smaller animals, badgers help to keep their populations from getting too large.

In some places, badgers are a **keystone species**. They are very important to their ecosystem.

Population

Overall, badger populations are **stable**. They are not **endangered**.

However, there are places where badger populations are **declining**. Badger populations have gotten so low in some places that they may become **extinct** there.

Badgers usually live between five and ten years. The oldest badger on record lived to be fourteen years old.

Badgers in Danger

Badgers are facing several threats. The main threat is habitat loss. Many badger habitats are being cleared for farmland, buildings, and roads.

With more roads through their habitats comes the threat of being hit by cars.

In some places, badgers are hunted by people who think they are pests.

Helping Badgers

Although badgers are not **endangered** in most places, there are ways that people are trying to help them.

In some places, there are special protected areas that provide animals like badgers with a safe habitat.

Some countries have laws that protect badgers from being hunted. In the United States, there are many places where badgers can only be hunted at certain times of year.

Laws like these protect badgers from **overhunting** while making sure that there are not too many badgers in the wild.

Glossary

Aggressive: mean, ready to fight

Chamber: room or compartment

Declining: getting smaller

Endangered: at risk of becoming extinct

Extinct: when there are no more of an animal left in the wild

Keystone Species: an animal that is very important to an ecosystem

Nocturnal: animals that are active at night

Omnivore: an animal that eats meat and plants

Overhunting: when too many of an animal are hunted and the population declines

Ridges: raised sections that are long and narrow

Solitary: living alone

Stable: unchanging, steady

Territory: an area of land that an animal claims as its own

Threatened: when an animal feels that it is in danger

About the Author

Victoria Blakemore is a first grade

teacher in Southwest Florida with a

passion for reading.

You can visit her at

www.elementaryexplorers.com

Also in This Series

Gray Wolves	Sloths	Flamingos	Camels	Koalas	Honey Bees	Pandas
Pangolins	White-Tailed Deer	Orcas	Giraffes	Corn	Meerkats	Echidnas
Walruses	Raccoons	Bald Eagles	Apples	Arctic Foxes	Red Pandas	Cassowaries
Tigers	Ladybugs	Moose	Beluga Whales	Leopards	Elephants	Jellyfish
Binturongs	Lions	Dolphins	Reindeer	Hammerhead Sharks	Hippos	Pumpkins
Peafowl	Chameleons	Florida Panthers	Aye-Ayes	Black Bears	Cheetahs	Manatees
Gingerbread	Polar Bears	Hot Chocolate	Orangutans	Coyotes	Marshmallows	Strawberries

Victoria Blakemore

Also in This Series

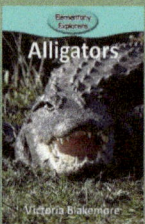

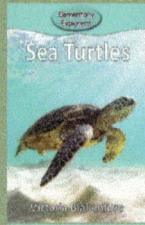

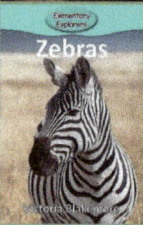

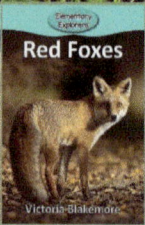

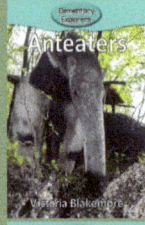

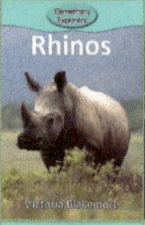

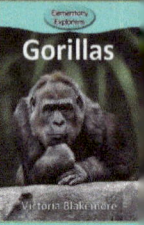

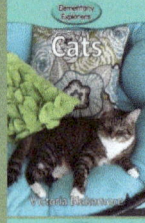

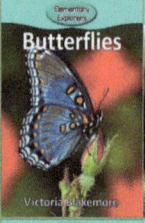

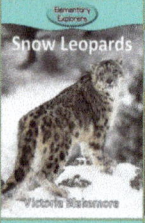

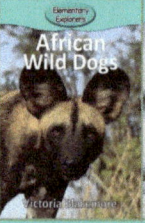

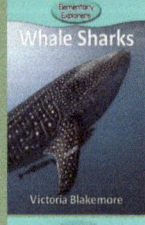

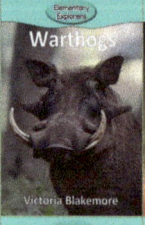

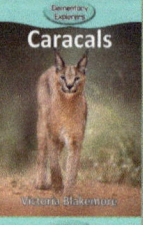

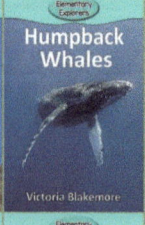

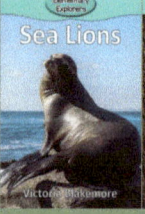

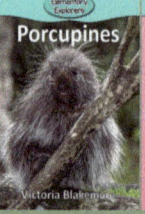

Aardvarks	Mako Sharks	Alligators	Frogs	Hedgehogs	Brown Bears	Bongos
Sea Turtles	Quokkas	Muskrats	Zebras	Red Foxes	Ring-Tailed Lemurs	Platypuses
Anteaters	Kangaroos	Rhinos	Jaguars	Wombats	Capybaras	Gorillas
Cats	Skunks	Butterflies	Dingoes	Snow Leopards	African Wild Dogs	Penguins
Whale Sharks	Wolverines	Warthogs	Caracals	Badgers	Seals	Hummingbirds
Pikas	Humpback Whales	Pumas	Lemonade	Llamas	Tulips	Ostriches
Sunflowers	Fennec Foxes	Sea Lions	Squirrels	Roses	Porcupines	Ice Cream

Victoria Blakemore

www.ingramcontent.com/pod-product-compliance
Lightning Source LLC
Chambersburg PA
CBHW051250020426
42333CB00025B/3146